A Gift For:

....

From:

....

How to Use Your Interactive Storybook & Story Buddy™:

1. Activate your Story Buddy™ by pressing the "On / Off" button on the ear.
2. Read the story aloud in a quiet place. Speak in a clear voice when you see the highlighted phrases.
3. Listen to your Story Buddy™ respond with several different phrases throughout the book.

Clarity and speed of reading affect the way Cooper™ responds.
He may not always respond to young children.

Watch for even more interactive Storybooks and Story Buddy™ characters.
For more information, visit us on the Web at www.Hallmark.com/StoryBuddy.

Copyright © 2011 Hallmark Licensing, Inc.

Published by Hallmark Gift Books,
a division of Hallmark Cards, Inc.,
Kansas City, MO 64141
Visit us on the Web at www.Hallmark.com.

Editors: Emily Osborn and Megan Langford
Art Director: Kevin Swanson
Designer: Mark Voss
Production Artist: Dan Horton

ISBN: 978-1-59530-353-0
KOB8002

Printed and bound in the United States

Hallmark
GIFT BOOKS

BOOK 2

Cooper's Rainy Day

By **Melvina Young** • Illustrated by **Crista Couch**

Cooper was a little bear who loved sunny days.
Playing outside was his very favorite thing.

What Cooper did NOT like were rainy days.
Other little bears liked playing in the rain
and splashing in puddles, but
Cooper did NOT want to do that.

One drip-droppy day,
Cooper tried counting raindrops
as they plinked and plopped
against the windowpane.
But that was not nearly as fun
as running, jumping, and climbing.
Cooper was bored.

"There are lots of things to do,"
Cooper's mom said.
"What about playing 'clean out
Cooper's messy closet'?"
"No!" grumped Cooper.
"Or how about 'pick up all
of Cooper's toys'?"
"No way!" he said.
Cooper did NOT want to do that!

"Why don't you go play with those old games in the attic?" his mom asked.
Cooper rolled his eyes but went to the attic to look around.
He saw some old skates and a bunch of baby toys—nothing worth playing with.

But then he saw it—the old TV box!
Cooper couldn't resist climbing inside.
As he did, he heard a giant rumble
of thunder, and suddenly . . .

TELEVISION BOX
HANDLE WITH CARE

UP   UP

. . . Cooper felt the box quake and shake.

TELEVISION BOX

HANDLE WITH CARE

ZOOM!

Cooper flew through space!
He raced past the moon. It glowed yellow
and looked like yummy cheese.
But there was no time to investigate.
Cooper's rocket ship moved so fast
that the stars zipped by.

Cooper flew farther and farther into outer space.
He went where no astrobear had ever been!
Cooper wondered if anyone lived way out here.
Just then an alien flew by in a UFO!

The alien and Cooper looked at each other in surprise.
Then they smiled and waved.
Traveling through the universe was a lot of fun, but
Cooper had other places to be.

SPLASH!

A water landing! Back on earth,
his spaceship turned into a submarine
and floated down deep into the ocean.
Everything was going along swimmingly
until a grumpy giant octopus tried to grab the sub.
With a few quick turns of the steering wheel,
Cooper got away just in time.

The water got bluer and bluer until it was almost black.
A whole school of glowing fish surrounded Cooper
and swam along with him as he toured the ocean floor.
Cooper waved good-bye as his sub climbed upward.
Exploring the ocean was fun, but
Cooper had other places to be.

BUMP!

Cooper's sub turned into a time machine—
and had just smacked into a giant tree
in the middle of a swampy forest!
He couldn't see much through the trees,
but he could see a huge Brontosaurus.
Cooper had a great idea.

Cooper tapped the huge dinosaur's toe and waved.
With a leafy grin, the Brontosaurus lowered her head,
and the little bear climbed up.
High into the sky rose Cooper!
He could see everything from up there!
Cooper felt like the king of the world!

Just then the ground rumbled, and Cooper heard a noise.

THUD . . . THUD . . . THUD!

"What was that?" Cooper slid down the dino's long neck
as the noise got closer and closer.

Whatever it was, it was big—and maybe dangerous.

Cooper ran back to his time machine.

THUD . . . THUD . . . THUD!

Cooper gulped. It must be a Tyrannosaurus rex!
Cooper sure hoped the T. rex wasn't in the mood
for a bear sandwich! Having lunch with a dinosaur?
Cooper did NOT want to do that!

THUD! THUD!

"Cooper!" Wait a minute—that wasn't a T. rex!
That was just Cooper's mom coming up the attic stairs!
Whew!
"The rain has stopped and the sun is shining," she said.
"Don't you want to play outside?"

Cooper smiled from inside the old TV box.
"That's okay, Mom," he said.
Cooper had other places to be!

DO YOU LOVE USING YOUR IMAGINATION LIKE COOPER™?
HALLMARK WOULD LOVE TO HEAR FROM YOU!

Please send your comments to:
Hallmark Book Feedback
P.O. Box 419034
Mail Drop 215
Kansas City, MO 64141

Or e-mail us at:
booknotes@hallmark.com